In the Lake of Your Bones

In the Lake of Your Bones

ა ઈ

Poems by
Peggy Dobreer

March 2012

In the Lake of Your Bones
© Copyright 2012 by Peggy Dobreer
All rights reserved. No part of this book may be used or reproduced in any manner whatsoever without written permission, except in the case of credited epigraphs or brief quotations embedded in articles or reviews.

Editors
Ricki Mandeville
Michael Miller

Graphic design
Michael Wada

Front cover art
Linda Vallejo

Back cover photo
Thom Sullivan

Moon Tide logo design
Ricki Mandeville

In the Lake of Your Bones
is published by
Moon Tide Press
Irvine, CA
www.moontidepress.com

Website designed by Mindy Nettifee and John Turi

FIRST EDITION

Printed in the United States of America

ISBN # 978-0-9839651-2-1

this book is for you

Contents

Foreword by Sarah Maclay   9

Decree   11

I.   *In the Silt*

Que Esta Queimando?   15
Full Frontal   16
Psalm of Mistaken Identity   17
Oh, India   18
Affinity   19
Nothing Is the Same   20
Architect of the Body   21
Gacela of Missed Appointment   22
Aubade   23
The Captain's Table   24
Le Prétendant   25
Apology   26
The Fabric of Man   27

II.   *In the Marrow*

De Nuestros Ojos   31
Backwards   32
Family Intervention   33
The Upper Room   34
Burn   35
In the Lion's Mouth   36
The Undifferentiated Aesthetic Continuum   37
First Love   38
Boss Lady   39
Felonious Activity   40
Technique   41
Layers   42
Color Me Gray   43
Reptilian Matters   44

III.   *In the Water*

Por el Amor de Dios	47
When Paint Hits Canvas	48
Across the Ribs of Red Canyon	50
The Lungs of My Planet	51
And What You Are Not	52
Unspoken	53
Aftermath	54
The Forever Under of It	55
Ode to an Organizing Query	56
Whispering the Question Later	57
In All Inglorious Visibility	58
A Recipe, My Love	59
Fledgling Humans We	60
Measures of the Heart	61
Full Moon Eclipse	62
Persuasions Lullaby	65
Acknowledgements	66
About the Author	67

Foreword

Inasmuch as this is a book of love poems—a book spoken joyously and wildly, dramatically and playfully, "shaking" its "core like a dirty / martini," to a specific and incarnate "you"—on another level, it is a book of love poems to longing—and even to the relief provided by our human ability to long. The heart's desert, after all, is not necessarily the skin's. And sometimes the hunger is not primarily for touch, but for the desire to touch—for desire itself. Both fulfillment and desire are staged in abundance here, as, in stages, we witness the opening of the heart in the language of the body—in this case, the body of a dancer acutely aware of the transformative power of contact, and the way everything—from mesa to sky to linguistic invention, "cowardice / of sugar, blue cave of tongue"—provides the shifting stage that shapes what the improv will become. Meanwhile, the dance itself pulls something unexpected from the dancer, something less focal in the fit of possession its narrative demands: however story turns out, what remains is the "magic" of an actual gift, no "hocus pocus." There could be an ending in "white paper . . . silver bells. " But even if "After the opera / a woman is bound in the wall," it will be a woman who has heard "a million laughing oceans, lucid and sacred," as well as felt the "weight of bone & dung"; a woman who can no longer forget that "Behind the wall is a breath . . ." It will be a dancer refreshed enough to remember the power of renewed attention to, hunger for, the fundamentals. Desire is one way to open the heart, "Technique," curiously, another. Because, as in the heart of this dance, whether in prose poem, gacela, aubade or addictive phrasing, metaphor, metonymy or ruffling, riffing, riffling list, "Always care of the floor comes first, as / breath falls to lower chakras, dissolves all / dissonance, light streams in . . ."

—Sarah Maclay

Decree

My love, you have the right
of first refusal. Everything
we say and trust will bend
like steel and hold like feathers.

If knowing all this you wish
to harvest the sky, open
your stars and let the moon
furnish your true name. No
harm will come from this.

I. In the Silt

"Thus saith the Lord to these bones..."
"Así dice el Señor a estos huesos..."
—Ezechiel 37:5

Que Esta Queimando?

after Other Side Camp

Everything. Everything is
burning, quiver and bow.
All things turquoise or pink,
held in a box with a fan on top.
Even the silk kimono is burning,
two cranes preening at the hem.
The shamisen, its body up in flames
even as the plucked note quarters,
even as a hand strums the belly.
And the fingers are burning, the lips,
even the thought that puckers the lips,
burning, all burning. The pout, the flush,
twisted ankle, knee where fluid once
collected. Parched, now ash. Burnt,
hot white. White as the salt flats,
white as the last breath taken.

Full Frontal

a still full moon
under cover and darkness
of midnight
the mere glance
of the orb
in my direction
flirts with duties
that lie before me
latches me into
its grasp tonight
it whets my appetite

I am night crawler
in my own skin
hovering alien
looking for prey
soft tissue vessel
carries fluid DNA
to inevitable rest
upon the hearth
a crafted nest

o, bury me
bury my head in your thigh
on your belly
lost in crook of neck
and slip of tongue
no absent glance
at the moon
but with full frontal
attention I thee wed
the still full moon
and my pen

Psalm of Mistaken Identity

I wish to write the poem that would chase
longing away. Would make desire a dark
roasted matter, meat eaten away, bones
white as prairie sand. I want the poem to
glisten on dirt, to wear distinction from
poppy fields to Timbuktu. I want the
gorges of Zanzibar to swallow every bite.

I wish to write the poem that says, my
only, only, forgive my every misstep,
greet each ghost with welcome. You will
shift-shape, billow into the luminous,
a million laughing oceans, lucid and sacred
like holy water—like art.

Oh, India

I listened to George Harrison
chant in Sanskrit,
until a wanderlust for Gujurat
pounced on me like a loose
litter of lion cubs.

I was smitten and stricken,
enamored and terrified,
walking through intentions of
passport acquisition and
frequent flyer's rejoice.

I was once a tiny monk,
maybe eight or nine lives old.
I was wrapped in mango robes,
freshly spun from my mother's loom.
I was walking contemplation, a view
from eyes in the back of the head,
looking in, unless and until,
looking through.

I was once a black-haired woman,
bent at the well for water. Mustard
flowers surrounded her head,
held the threads of her shawl
woven together. The colors
illuminated her charity.

I was once the vessel she held,
the one that gathered the water.
Om || *Asato Maa Sadgamaya* || *Om*
shantih: shantih: shantih: || She
was refreshment on the banks of
the Ganges, I was that gathering can.

Affinity

Calling all skins!

A set of turned down covers
        and the mockery

of a crack in
        the core of cerebellum

cannot contain
        the muscle of the heart

Breath becomes
        rock and roll short

becomes
        road to sin long

becomes for what
        you would

sacrifice all
        as you slide down

the final straw
        into something much larger

than your humiliation
        much longer than the exile of your Tibet.

Nothing Is the Same

"...all thy waves and billows have gone over me."
— Psalms 42:7

A ride along the coastline,
up the mountain, blackened hills,

valley in dismay. Four months later
everything is celadon and lace,

shoots on a cyclic entrance,
a Renaissance, turning of the moon.

Didn't we skip over tide pools,
moss giving wings to our tread?

Didn't we fall off compass,
get lost only to be found?

You are sheet lightning,
brazen like an elk,

beautiful color of doe,
tongue sharp as antler,

muscle buck of flank and snort,
white vapor of winter's mouth.

This poem is for you.

You are the sanctuary of these words.
Love learned in unsavory parables

gestates twin devotions. It's simple physics,
heart and matter. A well-wrought mantra,

hand of affirmation, the destiny of law.
What I wouldn't give for this truth.

The Architect of the Body

"first playground, last prison...sac to tote your runny vitals graveward."

—R. Selzer

This body dances the moon
do-si-dos the constellations
Ursa Major, Seven Sisters,
                      the dog star woofs
at the red pull of gravity
force of momentum
weight of bone & dung

This body bargains with crumbs
combs the thrift of unveiled
possessives   *his and hers, yours and ours*

and when sun enters center sky
physics calls to   *swing your partner*
please the orbit of planets
wink at dawn and meet
the horizon just so

This body is warmed against
the juniper   *way above the head*
reaches a platform of supplicants
a thousand steps   *to a new purview*

reveal of covert thighs
cross of ankles   *collision of breasts*
the curvature of biceps
burrows into elbow
industry of hand
to the flexion of foot

gray mass   *of what is known*
and that unknown

Gacela of Missed Appointment

I want the dark matter of night to stay all day
while embers of you comb through my hair.

I want your promise to ignite this cowardice
of sugar, blue cave of tongue.

Remember the horse of fire that rode between us
where plums fell and rivers were gods?

I want the succulent sword of you to split
this kiss of hawk — already on its way.

Aubade

                        I look
for remnants in my side drawer,
a mollusk, an errant sock, a book
of matches catches the eye. Once
there was a market for such items.
They reminded customers of what
the Buddha said, or the final words
of a prophet whose last request
is that you dance on his grave.
How can you refuse? The rain
of your loss runs down the cheek
of each *ronde de jamb*, each *piquet*.
Music disappears behind your bias
and the heel of your breath hits
the ground hard with every step.

                      A man's
name in *Devanagari* script is crisp
and treacherous. *Kali* guides every
dunda, with the instinctual caution
of a lioness with cubs. His footsteps
creep across the crepe of night, abrupt
as any leave taking, weather disturbing
the evidence, changing its hue.

The Captain's Table

the ocean's brood is the foam at its edge
the candor in the deep of its broth

It swallows you swell by swell.

predators slide through the ooze
each nub rides up against the other

>	the stingray
>	the manatee
>	the monk

When you learn it is a river.
Learn it has gills.

neighbors all

>	in cruelty of fisher's net
>	stain of squid
>	mercury lurking in briny crude

Near harbor of sleep.

a submarine pierces the aqueous bark

>	divides the knowing sea
>	fish scatter out of school
>	the bough is lifted until...

Pond of your eye.

...wave walls drop out from under
and a candle on the captain's table blows out

You drown describing it

Le Prétendant

The last time I saw a cock fight
I was in Cambodia. But I don't remember
going to Cambodia.

And why would I have gone? I'm not
in the military, no particular fondness
for the region, no familial connection.

Now talk about Kasmir, or Java, or Tibet,
but Cambodia? Listen. I am want for
tablas in my blood, vedas in my ear.

I am peaks of Pradesh, Prapto's dance
among the ruins, silk of a billion saris
prostrate on temple floors.

Marble incense. Ascetic swoon.
Luxury lures in practice of Asteya,
Brahmacharya.   Aum.
Love reclines on the bottom rung.

A prompt that leads like Shakyamuni's
mother, like Jesus in a rain forest,
like standing alone on Mt. Nanda Devi

in the dark glow of a blue moon. Faller.
No chute. Climber without rope. *Shut
your stars and stay clear. Be only this.*

Apology

As the year of the lemur draws to a close
and midnight settles on a windstorm
of error, if you're looking for proof of my
coarse nature, here it is. Slammed against
egregious acts I have committed with
my violin upon the weary shinbone
of your sensitivities. I am a parsimonious
porch, wrapped around the house of your generosity.
Please accept this crucible, these apologetic suds
to cleanse the very arteries of any wrongdoings
which I may have delivered upon your house
while splayed against the burnt sienna sky.

The Fabric of Man

O the obstinate plaid
the deep breath of linen
saturnalia of silk
the cornfields of cotton
pandemonium of tulle
the falsehood of polyester
pantomime of lace
the savagery of wool
caustics of vinyl
the holy shit of fine leather
compassion of bamboo
the neon colors of yarn
handspun from the discarded
saris of the aristocracy
the war of the senses
fought over the cowardice
of a camouflage jacket
an overture in the B flat
of anguish opera's heavy
velvet curtain as it falls

II. In the Marrow

"As a dancer desists from dancing, having exhibited herself to the audience, so does Primal Nature desist, having exhibited herself to the spirit."
—Sāmkhya Karika LIX

De Nuestros Ojos

After the opera
a woman is bound in the wall.
One window looks in, another
looks out.
The uninvited one calls
for silence.
That's how you'll know it's begun.
She will nod with conviction,
and run.
She runs like a girl,
but she's fast.

Backwards

From the bay window on Fillmore
you can reach out and grab the wires.
You can fry on metro lines if you want,
from the flat above the fluff and fold.

But good is the smell of fresh-pressed
cotton, perfect crisp. You can jump a cable car,
grab a strap, ride the wind to the wharf
where the air is pungent. You can shop
for leather, get things pierced, you can dangle
your boots over the side, forget about lunch,
notice your scarf flying behind in reflections
on the inside edge of your shades.

Some things are too close for comfort, so
you take off lenses, close your lids to the sky,
let the salt spray refresh you, let it bind you to this
freedom, let it mimic the hand you used to hold.

Family Intervention

1.
Mother was a fragile moment,
a leaky valve. A crimson song not sung
at bedtime. Actually, she never hummed
at all. But she loved a good combo.
Could fox trot with pizzazz.

2.
Father was double vision memory,
over and over on yellow pages.
Or else a dancer made of enamel,
a purple pendant that was worn
for a tango or a waltz.

3.
My brother was a broken arm
I believed was contagious and wouldn't
let him touch me. My hair gathered in
a bun that made my eyes slant at nine.

4.
The puppy came home in a shoebox,
a ribbon around her neck
like a noose. A tiny teacup,
we all thought she was a rodent.
Searched relentlessly under the pup's
rump for a longer tail.

5.
When father took off his belt, the great
avocado tree held up its branches to
block the buckle from splitting the lip
of the sky. And my favorite cat, François
Villon, sat on a ledge like mercury, purring.

The Upper Room

On the second story is a room that opens into a closet
bigger than the room itself.

On the second story is a window, round,
that suggests a submarine or a T-Bird, 1958.

On the second story I peep down on the patio —
boys and girls slow dancing,

the Five Stairsteps and Supremes, drinking Tab and High C.
On the second story is a bedroom, dresser hiding lingerie, silk ties.

On the second story, bars were installed too late.
A thief climbed the trellis, opened the window, took everything

that wasn't nailed down. Nothing left but a single bed
with a canopy, even the bunny gone from the pillow.

Burn

The brick incinerator behind the back house was where I learned to play with fire. The ground was covered in ivy. Vines ran down the chimney and the chain-link fence along the edge of our property, leaves big as a man's hand. You could barely get through. A cast iron door swung on crusty hinges, eroded from the heat of fire to ash: tissue, newsprint, TV dinner packages, and featherless birds who fell from nests in the yard. They went in too. The year they made it illegal to burn trash within city limits small brush fires broke out everywhere. Sirens were heard two, three times a week, most by the creek, near the whitewashed bridge. That was long before global warming, long before the fox was driven so far back into the hills.

In the Lion's Mouth

My birth was strung between two wars
Like a hammock in a hot tornado
They say she left us to leave him

Because his eyes were full of shrapnel
He surrendered to the metal
My birth was strung between two wars

No one knows who fed and clothed us
Containment caused him to re-enlist
They say she left us to leave him

Once escaped the *lion's mouth*
who dares goes in again?
My birth was strung between two wars

His B-29 Superfortress Bombardment
Wing burst into flames on take-off
They say he left us to leave her

His 100th mission was to be his last
The whole crew lost to the Okinawa sea
They say she left us to leave him
My birth was strung between two wars

The Undifferentiated Aesthetic Continuum

I am winner of a blue ribbon for my thinking.
No one gets it, but they find me entertaining.
When the award was presented, a crow perched
on a telephone pole and bombarded the ceremony
with loud caws. The bird was uncanny in remarks
punctuated to utterly disturb the proceedings. I was
completely upstaged by the one-note winged one.
While we waited for the raven to quiet, jasmine
blossoms scented the afternoon and when I looked
up there was a sleek silver cylinder moving high across
the sun, and three swooping crows winding low.
The loud bird had gone. Then I remembered. Legend
says, *when the owl speaks, someone dies*. If someone else
has died today, I have not been notified. But Aung San Suu Kyi
has been released and a little win for peace has come
under the watchful eye of the flock.

First Love

The rhythm of my blood
beats along the river of my being.

The joy of motion lifts my leg
and tosses it into the air,

follows the sensation of each foot
on the ground. Gravities embrace.

Tears must roll down cheeks
for spirits to lift again. And arms,

they are lifted into gesture. Look!
It's Lord Shiva swaying to the spin

of Earth on her axis. Rise up. Hear
voices of angels. Rise up. Set yourself free.

Feel sun on your face and wind at your heels.
Know that when you hold your lover in grass

at dawn, you can gaze into the soil, hear fossils
breathe. Here is the now and forever. Here

is the falling into grace. Here is the rapture of
a poem as it moves across my face.

Boss Lady

She waited in the plaza of Old Town Santa Fe.
Wanted to feed the pigeons but had no bread.
A purple draped Jesus adorned St. Francis Chapel.
Molé still burned in her mouth like the friction off
a Christmas train in a souvenir shop. Her maiden
name was all she had. That, and a linen bridesmaid dress,
empire waist, lace over bodice. Worn to run bricks
from TJ to Anaheim in the trunk of daddy's Cadillac.
She'd wrap the evidence in white paper with silver bells.
Take the top down, bouquet of yellow roses on the seat,
hair scraping against the sky.

Felonious Activity

This is what it is when a hand
reaches in and grabs your throat
tosses you into yourself like an ache
a barrel of worms eating you out
leaving a lattice of toil.

This is what it is when faith
fails to turn presumptions over.
Shouts sprout outside your window.
Hot winds blow against the screen.
This is the hour of swallows returning.
A blended quagmire of wings against
the foothills shades the crops below.

This is a move closer to breast, nearer
to belly, shaking your core like a dirty
martini, leaving you heaped on the floor,
stopped mid flight, hand still firmly
wrenched around your throat, angry marks
rising on your perfectly perfumed neck.

Technique

A dancer walks down Mission Street
with a Marlboro in one hand and a
latte from La Bohème in the other.
She is a rainbow muffler around thorax,

warming calves, pumping smoke,
dragging deep into the celery snap of
another San Francisco morning, and
itching to pull on the day's first leotard.

This is Mariposa, heart of the dance.
A cable car up Polk, bus across town,
stop at the café and half a mile hoofing
it into the warehouse district.

Industrial doors open to cement hallways,
open to studio spaces softened by
sprung wood floors. The smell of
kiln and oils, and the long push of

a cotton broom across caramel floors.
Always care of the floor comes first, as
breath falls to lower chakras, dissolves all
dissonance, light streams in through

southern exposure. Today, the spirit of
Erick Hawkins wields the broom. Footsteps
are a barely audible imprint on the ear,
so quiet you can hear your breath.

Layers

The snake had shed its skin a few
days before I arrived. The snake
was active, more active than I had
ever seen it. He said it was because
the snake had just shed its skin.
He said it twice.

He wasn't standing in his usual place
when I got off the elevator. He was
closer to it. I almost knocked him over
trying to get to his usual place but
he was closer to the elevator,
waiting for me.

His mother had sent Georgia peaches
preserved in jars. They had just arrived
that day. He wanted me to taste them.
He was hungry, hungry like the snake,
closer to the elevator, more active
than I had ever seen him.

Color Me Gray

The boundaries of my world mingle with hers.
One house, one home…two hearts entrained
by proximity and the absence of intrusion. She was
fashioned from my flesh. Now, we have been
delivered in a spin onto the platform of her
approaching self.

She is champing at the bit, ready to mount
the carousel of next exploration, jumping on
at any given moment. I am loath to stand
outside the lines. Color me gray when things
appear too black and white in her world. She
never seems to give much information.

The golden threads of her childhood to my
mystical marsupial pouch are frayed. She is
stepping away. Her culture holds the needs
of mine in contempt. I am ancient, dim witted
in her mind. She is magnificent, fearless, and
fragile in mine. I would swaddle her for comfort
and protection but my arms no longer reach
around her widening expectation.

I am crackling, slow-walking, back-looker. She
is fired up peeling into tomorrow, only
present to just what is at hand, even
changing direction at the very moment of inception.
Nothing is consistent, love is constant.

I am obsolete. She is invention. I am polarized.
She is all systems go, leaping forward, throwing
down, full throttle, wide open. I am hands folding
in my lap. Much as I am able, I am letting go.

Reptilian Matters

He named his lizard after me,
a crusty, darting creature. I
looked for recognition of this
comparison in someone's eyes,

but saw none. He kept the lizard
on the back porch where it was drafty.
This was further disturbing to me,
namesake of an ostracized reptile.

His father, on the other hand,
named a kitten after me. He was
a judge, a gentle man. He sat
on the bench by profession.

People looked up. He purred
into my ear when we danced.
The kitten came back to my house,
purred into my lap all night.

III. In the Water

*"I sing myself into a pearl…
roll into the open mouth of the Divine."*
— Ruth Forman

Por el Amor de Dios

we morph to skin and bone
we soar now taxi down
glades of cloud and cluster breath

time is a blanket of mesa
takes claim on masks of the body
we morph to skin and bone

we write with rhythmic dust
lift curtains we descend through
glades of cloud and cluster breath

prana glows in vestibules
curls around the nettle sprig
we morph to skin and bone

we are fish at home in the Wadden Sea
say what the pot bellied moon won't say
glades of cloud and cluster breath

a certain bite of indigo
is met at canyon's edge
glades of cloud and cluster breath
we morph to skin and bone

When Paint Hits Canvas

On the side of the brain
that knows no logic she
finds her way each night
to his door. He is the hope
of soldiers returning,
the mercy of rounds
emptied in her own defense.

On the side of the brain
that dances without reserve
her card is crowded with the
letters of his name. His fragrance
floats on her hair.

On the side of the brain
that hosts kaleidoscopes of light
around the moon, she is made
of glass, translucent as rain.
He can see right through her.
She is a clear stream where
only he may drink.

On the side of the brain
where paint hits canvas and
breaks up darkness, she is
cross cut to perfection, a
sapphire without inclusion,
made bezeled and bound.

On the side of the brain
where night calls in wonder
and day looks for darkness
they meet in the country of misses
and flares. They are roadside
warnings come in triplicate,
stunted by numbers. Just go ahead,
say they're guilty, they won't deny it.

On the side of the brain where
sand touches satin and photographs
are surreal as time or science,
they are catalogues of creative urges,
candid shots to museum collections,
they are post election polls, they go
beyond the limits of our reach. They
teach the bounty of their difference,
they are mercy and infantry, paradigms
colliding in collective drive. They are alive
when paint hits canvas. Then, they die.

Across the Ribs of Red Canyon

at the mercy of planets
rants in bold letters echo
through layers where a river
once birthed a teeming *bosque*
ran so full it punctured rock
jutting around the next cliff
there's a cherry tree explosion
giant script stippled of orchards
misplaced in a moistless landscape
sweet white blooms wet on emerald
fittings merge at impossible junctures
as kindly as two submissive moons
orbiting ever without implosion
volunteers grow from shale rock
survive to deny any absence of
blossoms O sing wayward comet
stay alive in a merciless sky

The Lungs of My Planet

My love is rainforest dense.
Caught in the understory,
machetes are needed to free
the fire. My love is a canopy,
lichen teeming with creatures
that imitate native tongue.
His voice cracks under the vine.
He is vicious in his kindness,
absent of vows. He is the glow
of lodge rocks when they first come in.
Sparks that fritter on spots where copal lands.
The hiss of water gone blessed as it pours.

And What You Are Not
after Billy Collins

You are the nib and the ink.
You are parchment calling at dawn.
As light wavers, you are vapor escaping the room.

And surely, you are the winterberry,
your brambles stick and sting.
And look, now you are a mailbag.

You are the invitation, the limousine,
and the note that offers thanks. But you are
not the firefly, nor the bear in the room.

You are neither the bane nor the balm.
And you are absolutely not the Milagros
lost in a dry field outside of Tucson.

But I am the mission, and I am the bell. I am
the fry bread on the truck in the field. I am adobe
and brick, and you are the mortar that binds.

You are the shining salt of a sparkling parable.
You are the horse and you are its blinders.
You are a chariot turning, for heaven's sake

and make no mistake, you are the best
of the wheel. You are the spoke and the hub.
And I am a smooth gray stone on the road.

Unspoken

I want to tell you that one lifetime will never be enough,
the red mountain calls my name lost between our worlds.
I could go there with you and never come back.

I want to show you the way I curl into you under quilts,
the way shots roar through galaxies where there is only you.
I want to say I need you, the way you need heat,

the way crime needs a victim, the way Saturn needs a ring.
I want to say it all, from the first ache to the rage
of each refusal, want to carry you in the folds

of my skirts, twirl you on porches to music that no one
else hears, dance with you in the kitchen while wild rice
simmers on the stove. I want to hold you from the cellar

of my fear to the attic of all we know to be true, want to be
true as I never have, as sure as the wheel must turn,
as certain as God's eye in communion's cup.

I want to cherish you always, going about my given plan,
shower you in mango and lime, dry you with fingertips hot
with the stains of my sin. Want to roll you like Persian carpet

and ship you home. I want to start all over, be
the Christmas of our youth. Would that I could,
and that it pleased you like nothing before.

Aftermath

It's a simple act
of lift and conquer,
hunt and gather,
unleash and protect.

Subdivide the very marrow
of your bones. Let sugar
run from your lakeside
and scoop into clouds.

The vector of chance may
incite planetary madness.
Take cover under the moon, my love.
Save your thoughts till I arrive.

I will read your algorithms,
elements all in order,
each array a binary prediction.
I am of textbooks and rain.

I know your name.
My scaffold is a chaos
of nonexistent zeros,
folds me to my knees.

The Forever Under of It

After things have been said badly
a pervasive calm falls on the house.
Oxidation rises like an unrelenting bruise
that colors everything.

Even sun holds little glare, barely catches
the light off the hills. Very few notice
gooseflesh rising, or the light rifting
in a distant room, embers dying, chill

coming in through the lace of winter's coat.
It's not the settling on the ear that counts
but the lifting of the gate. A truth can tarnish
even finest metal, leave porosity, burn

away compounding evidence. Filigree,
our interlaced necessities on ice.

Ode to an Organizing Query

"Maybe the only perfect thing in life is longing."
—Marie-Elizabeth Mali

There is a question on the tip.
It can wait like peeling bark, but
won't. You have to know by now.

What's carved in can be read.
An offering is a branch. Scuttles
the sky with cupped palm open.

Holy water pools in crevices,
time seeps out like mercury.
Longing wins again.

Whispering the Question Later

A voice sings itself quiet,
murders perfect syllables.
Used to be sure of the tone
before the rigging of ties,
before the felling of finds,
before knowing landing
more often than flight.
Quiets itself at the shore.
Prays on a pier
of inescapable creosote.
Behind the wall is a breath,
sprig of Spanish moss,
the croak of evergreen,
and a back porch
with a milk deposit chamber
near the door.

In All Inglorious Visibility

I called your name because
I dreamt I was vanishing.
An erosion of thoughts that
once held up under scrutiny.
I dreamt you held me, were
all I needed, bone to bristle,
word to wonder of flight.
The lip of synchronicity
laps at the edges of our rooms,
rich water wets the coil,
wrapping up inductions.
My right hip melts into yours.
Our bones are wisdom walking.
We are filled for brewing, over
flowing, our cup holds a clinic
of doubt, casts one infinite
notion to the hot held wind.
How to say the things we have
no right to say? How to stand
still in our own eyes, become
visible? How to coax the Sandias
back to our front door?

A Recipe, My Love

It's the cribbed curry that will not leave
the tongue, that reaches past the stove's
hot breath, extols savory ingredients.
Cardamom feeds the empty leg and flavors
a meal of condiment and extract. Almond
oil spreads across the back of night,
a place to sit that fits like a Thanksgiving
suture, sewing the stars inside your palms.
tatting the moon in my hair.

Fledgling Humans We

the unruliness of my clock face,
 my breath, my sharp claw, let worlds come
all together, signs empathic, foreheads collide,
 we are meant for this

We become food at the table
A sawed-off barrel falls deep
Comes right back when drawn up
Our skin melts in the heat of afternoon
I have caused this chasm of canyons
This dining car rides rails of extinction
Raw meat hangs on a hook

Sympatic powders have been found
There is elasticity in my thoracic cavity
You mustn't say you've seen it if you never have
It's either magic or it's just hocus pocus

This is a crabgrass contemplation
Instead say your name Face your mantra
in a singular drop of myrrh Cover your head
Let the honey run Let it be holy
Let it suckle at every pore of you
Every seed every fluid every vice
Let it render a fierce Durgha
on the walls of your cave Let it wade
in the lake of your bones read you
in adequate light cover to cover looking
up every unfamiliar word as you go

Measures of the Heart

"When he became too large to hide, she made a basket of bulrushes and sealed it."
—Exodus: 3.1

Please, report lost or stolen items
right away, day or night.
Use your PIN with caution.
Refrigerate to avoid spoiling
but only after cracking the seal.
Peel one perfect grape. And if
you already know how sutures feel
why mention them….why ask at all?
Why rub daisies on riverbeds?

Rather, turn the dial three times right, one
to the left, and two right again. Numbers
thereafter will fall with ease
on the Fibonacci ratio. They will fret
like old men who have gathered their salt,
who still remember the briny down
of the sea…or the ripe Bulrushes of Tulare.

Full Moon Eclipse

In waking you preside. I am
nestled in the cloud of your last thought,
your easy words, how they echo—

—ho. The way they roll off the verb
of your élan. The jawbone of a whale
begins to hum inside my breath.

The way a lunar eclipse approaches,
dreams us in red, says *distraction dies
as seeking is sated.* Come

see the brow of morning, ignite
one portal this perishable hour.
Is that you in the loam?

The orb darkens crimson
till only her white apron returns—
—luminous above rooftops.

Look at me while amaranth
cradles the sky. I am the night
lake of your bones.

afterthought

Persuasions Lullaby

The braiding of two songs
on a beach or a chain gang.
Bottom notes of an intifada
at play in desire's dark night.

Let the tones come up. Heads
bobbing at the surface. A lake
or a blue moon, there is
no glass bottom, no oar.

Nothing to be tied down, no
dock on the harbor. Only
fruit left out to ripen. Only
juice runs as pomegranate

cracks open to small morsels, bright
as blood hits air flow river of
sustenance. O, let the bones
of the berries stick in your teeth.

Acknowledgements

The author wishes to thank or acknowledge these journals and chapbooks in which the following poems have appeared, sometimes in an earlier version:

※

Little Captures, **First Eyes Press:** "Oh, India," "Nothing Is the Same," "The Captain's Table," "First Love," "Technique," "Backwards," "Felonious Activity," "Layers," "Reptilian Matters"
Face of Sky, **First Eyes Press:** "Full Frontal," "Affinity,"
Malpais Review, **Gary Brower:** "In the Lion's Mouth"
Mas Tequila Press, **Richard Vargas:** "Aubade"
Duke City Fix, **Jon Knudsen:** "Across the Ribs of Red Canyon"
Don't Blame the Ugly Mug: 10 Years of 2 Idiots Peddling Poetry, **Ben Trigg and Steve Ramirez:** "Persuasions Lullaby"
www.foggedclarity.com: "Que Esta Queimando?"

※

A very special thanks:
To Brendan Constantine for his generous mentorship and inspiration, and words from "The Merman's Kiss" in the Cento, "The Captain's Table"; to Linda Vallejo for her practical and spiritual guidance, and her artwork on the cover of this book; to Mariano Zaro and Richard Garcia, who assisted with early edits; to Michael Miller, Moon Tide Press, for believing in this manuscript, and Ricki Mandeville for tending to its detail; to my daughter, who always gets to make the first cut; and to all who have inspired and supported this work. Thank you so much.

About the Author

Peggy Dobreer came to poetry by way of dance and experimental theater. Her work appears in such journals as *Malpais Review, San Pedro River Review, WordWrights Magazine* and *LA Yoga*, and is widely anthologized. In 2005 she founded the now legendary Horse of Another Color series. Peggy lives in Los Angeles with her daughter. You may visit her at *www.peggydobreer.com* for details or contact.

Patrons

Moon Tide Press would like to thank the following people for their support in helping to publish the finest poetry from the Southern California region. To sign up as a patron, visit www.moontidepress.com or email publisher@moontidepress.com.

GOLD PATRONS

Gayle K. Brunelle
Peggy Dobreer
Michael Kramer
Karen Billman Lucas
Robert and Michele Miller
Felice Newman
Gail Newman
Orange Lutheran High School
Viorela Pop
Bill Rogers
Rachanee Srisavasdi
Tom and Pamela Tellez
G. Murray Thomas
Dayana Vazquez

PATRONS

Brad and Patricia Hachten
Jack and Consuelo Marshall
John Perry

Also Available from Moon Tide Press

Lost American Nights: Lyrics & Poems, Michael Ubaldini
March 2006

Tide Pools: An Anthology of Orange County Poetry
June 2006

Sleepyhead Assassins, Mindy Nettifee
September 2006

A Thin Strand of Lights, Ricki Mandeville
December 2006

Kindness from a Dark God, Ben Trigg
June 2007

Carving in Bone: An Anthology of Orange County Poetry
December 2007

A Wild Region, Kate Buckley
April 2008

In the Heaven of Never Before, Carine Topal
December 2008

Now and Then, Lee Mallory
December 2009

Pop Art: An Anthology of Southern California Poetry
May 2010

What We Ache For, Eric Morago
October 2010

One World, Gail Newman
March 2011

Hopeless Cases, Michael Kramer
July 2011

I Was Building Up to Something, Susan Davis
November 2011